T0337668

Inside the Yellow Dress

Mary Ann Samyn

New Issues Poetry & Prose

A Green Rose Book

New Issues Poetry & Prose
The College of Arts and Sciences
Western Michigan University
Kalamazoo, Michigan 49008

An Inland Seas Poetry Book

 Inland Seas poetry books are supported by a grant from
The Michigan Council for Arts and Cultural Affairs.

First Edition, 2001

ISBN: 1-930974-09-4 (paperbound)

Library of Congress Cataloging-in-Publication Data:
Samyn, Mary Ann
Inside the Yellow Dress/Mary Ann Samyn
Library of Congress Catalog Card Number: 2001131155

Art Direction: Tricia Hennessy
Design: Shane Dubay
Production: Paul Sizer
                   The Design Center, Department of Art
                   College of Fine Arts
                   Western Michigan University
Printing: Courier Corporation

Inside the Yellow Dress

Mary Ann Samyn

New Issues

WESTERN MICHIGAN UNIVERSITY

Also by Mary Ann Samyn

Captivity Narrative

For G

Contents

V. There was a glimmer of it

VI. This is sweet too–

Like human skin . . . cloth is a membrane that divides an interior from an exterior. It both reveals and conceals.

—Ann Hamilton, *whitecloth*

Inside the Yellow Dress

Inside the Yellow Dress (1)

—It got worse and worse until I couldn't put two words together: for example, *pony tail*, each part rearing up, wanting to be the main thing. But the main thing was the ribbon, which I wanted but didn't mention for fear of angering the other words. Also the scissors, which lay on the dresser, admiring themselves in the mirror. *I better not* became my theme. As in childhood, when I was easily bribed by a little candy: the slightest nod or lemon drop.

I

Do you know subtraction?

—Backward glance:

this is the look of a wish

just before it dissolves:

a sweet airy nothing—

Like angels, maybe.

Surely you have folded your body down:

here's the church and here's the steeple—

Of course you were *less than*,

but also *better than.*

Isn't that how suffering works?

first you crouch down . . .

Entering the Text

So the page is a field—

        wildflowers, roadside

and I want to pull over,
I want to get out of the car.

Remember—? We did this once,
stopping for something blue along a fence

        —was it wisteria?

and you picked some
and you offered it to me.

~

This is how it starts:
you have to make an offering,
you have to bring a blessing with you
wherever you go—

~

A field like a room.
As in, where is the door to this field?

        —Oh, of course!
        the scent of wisteria—

~

And you thought I had forgotten
that whatever we bless
in the world blesses us.

~

Not *a* but *the*,
as in this particular field,
which is the poem we're in just now,
chicken wire along the perimeter
come loose here and there.

~

The question is: should we climb over
or crawl right through?

~

So this is an offering
or doorway:

the poem's tall grasses
brushing your bare limbs

                    —can you feel that?

And the scent of wisteria

                         —is it on your hands now?

Moving Away from an Event

—So I am thinking of Chinese lanterns.
    —no. I mean the plant,
    the orange husks.

Because I could not have them
    (they were in someone else's yard;
    I was not brave enough),

I wanted them   more.

    —but more than what?

More than I would have imagined.

It is always like this.
I cannot calculate
the hurt ahead of time.
I cannot spare myself.

        So I go headlong—

I go wanting.

And these flowers:
        how bright they are.
Dried,
    they keep their color all winter.

November

In the middle of the middle
the thing resists, will not be written.

So I make a circle, stamp about,
clumsy bootprints in the snow.
And I step outside—

Call this perspective.
Though it isn't.
Though I'm incapable,
inconsolable, inside   still.

But who can describe an interior:
yellow leaves beneath the snow—?

I have tried and tried.
I have called this "my project"
as though to distance—

I have said the bare branches
are fine with me,
                    just fine.

I have said

                    the loss is exquisite—

Poem with a Riddle in It

—So I said OK, I will crawl under the hurt
the way I dreamed my mother beneath the fir tree:

She's gone and she's not coming back—

This is what I said and knew:
that there was a staircase and she took it,
that I saw her go.

~

To be in this body is hard enough. I cannot imagine another.

~

In second grade she began to worry:

If God is good, then He would not abandon us.
If heaven is happiness, it must be safe.
If only someone would meet us halfway—

~

Like a rope and bucket.

(one of us coiled, one of us—)

Like twilight.

(Yes, holes. Yes, riddled with—)

~

There were vowing and non-vowing angels.
That much she had figured out.
Also, that the story of Adam asleep
was troublesome.

                    After all, who would steal a rib and why?

~

My mother is anger and want, a small girl.
I am a small girl too.
One of us darts in and out of the bushes.

                    The other cannot imagine her suffering.

Private Tunnel (3)

When I go back, my foot catches in the jaw:
its shape and sound.

This is the third time I am trying to explain
the danger of occurring *live*

like newscasters on TV:
who can predict the outcome?

Now as before,
green and yellow dime store birds fill this space,

dirty tufts of feather in my hair
like the silent *after* of confetti.

When I slip from my shoe,
I mean to postpone it:

Here I am! I say,
mother—, feed on this—

Self-Portrait as an Animal Skinned and Hung

Or as her. Or as her hands, the little—
how can I say this?—flicking—no,
bobbing, the fingers do this nervous thing
because—now listen, are you listening?
she never quite seems to be—and I need
to explain it right and relax into
the into because then the skinning part
might not be so—oh, I don't know—
chop chop, I guess, and the boundaries,
you know, the let's call this x or me or
whatever, and let's call this other mess
y—remember?—hasn't that been
quite the riddle?—hasn't she always said
you never can tell you just never can.

Voice Box

1

When I climbed the chair, what I wanted was the littlest box,
the bit of brilliance I knew my mother had hidden there—

> (her ring,
> or some
> small thing,
> some part
> of her)

Can you imagine it, the little box, felt and bordered
like a poem by white space, faraway as her voice
in home movies, close as right now, as mine—?

2

Her voice is *the ability to.*
Her voice is *the specified quality.*
Her voice is *the medium or agency.*
Her voice is *the right or opportunity.*
Her voice is so young on the phone
she could be me, all my friends say—

3

It began when I did.

It lingers because it's inside.

It calls my name in our voice.

(All this could be in response
to my therapist's first question:

so, how are you like your mother?,
which even now I miss-type as *mouther*)

4

Definition 11 is: *an awkward or perplexing situation; predicament.*

In other words, I found *this* box instead.

In other words, *here I am!*

5

—But when I chose to voice

(*to utter, to pronounce,* to poem)

I knew what would happen:

saying, *see how she runs,*

pointing to the white around her—

6

So how cruel am I?

utter utter

The word means *complete, absolute, entire*

as though all along

I just pretended

I didn't put the cut in the side of the maple

(it was that kind of box too, except—)

pretended I didn't hover at her larynx,

didn't want the sweet part to flow out,

so that I might fret about it,

so that I might collect it—

I could keep it low —

—Just another little minute,

       as my mother would say

  in her sweet pleading.

Like a lamb,

    I always thought—

curls you could run your hand through

      though dirty maybe. Frisky.

But who wouldn't want a tuft

  —all edges, but soft to finger—

who could resist the warm breath,

      the bleating

      of a clean hunger—

Bog

Having been tame for so long

    (pet deer, nice eyes)

anger required too much pushing *into*—
My wrists ached.

Even when I tried, said

    The woods are full of bad adjectives,
    but I am brave, etc.

Even when I thought I could be
mostly (fill-in-the-blank)
and just a little *not*—

Even when *best luck* fell at my feet,

                     I let it—

Self-Portrait as the Wallpaper with Little Stoves

You'd think smoke.
You'd think curling from me.

But it's not like that.
My mouth is not.

Mostly, nothing occurs.
Of course there are little shovels

for the coal, and a wheelbarrow
with a squeaky wheel.

But mostly I pretend.
For example, long ago.

Or, I have walked all day
and my cheeks are flushed.

Poem of Interrupted Charm

—All day, I had prayed to be better,
saying *Please God,*

    don't let me shut down—

This was the not-feeling day, a 1920s "sweet shoppe"
named after Diana, huntress, goddess of charm,
goddess of the velvet rope.

 ~

This was October, Port Huron,
and the brochure promised pastries and candy,
a "delicious display," the restaurant
untouched, the big copper pot the very same one:

  uninterrupted charm

     —imagine that—

        since 1926.

 ~

No one knows where I am!
was my happy thought, earlier,
as I walked along the water,
freighters drifting by and Canada
exactly where it always is:

     just close enough.

 ~

The space between me and everything else—

 for example: any *you*

is like the space between sentences in a prose poem:

so much happens—

like Tennessee,

      the road cut into the mountains:

yes, beautiful,

      but steep on each side,

and around each curve,

         another—

~

When G returned, he held my face
and I asked its shape.

Pentagonal, he said.

As though I am the government, that complicated.
As though he could get lost in a bad way,

      was what I thought.

No, he said, just complex,
his hands on me still,

      his eyes—

~

When I looked up *charm* in the dictionary,
I knew I was not pleasing.

~

Later we watched astronauts get strapped in,
the space shuttle taking off over and over.

The whole day was this way:

      near and *far* all mixed up.

~

Also, the idea of *outer space* struck me as funny,
as I lay awake,

farther and farther inside—

~

The problem was how to locate charm:

For example, was it in the glass cases at the sweet shoppe,
rows and rows of candy necklaces,
my mirrored face?

Was it that string and sugar part of me wanted

just to have a little luck,

for once,

a little something fine—?

I'll Take This and This

Always you want more.
First space, then something to fill it up:
little snip of bone, St. Anne's,
against the brown cloth
no one has touched in so long.
And the air inside?
Not warm as his breath at your neck,
not shifting and delicate.
But rancid, all but forgotten—

A Career Guide for Girls

—Then the question behind the other questions:

Are you "service
                    oriented"—?

                              (Are you a hot or cold beverage?)

In other words, here are your choices:
teacher nurse stewardess,
some helping
profession, some *oh you*

        poor thing you—

                    is there anything I can—

        Sir—?

NoNoNo
This is not your big brave famous—,
                                        is it?

        Oh, come on now.

She left suddenly is what they'll say
if you don't tell.

            She flinched   south.

As though you weren't oriented
                    properly.

As though you couldn't manage
a compound
you.

For example: home + maker
or   house + wife

Such nice words!

As though the oven loves you.   (the red coil: *hiss hiss*)

As though the Early American wallpaper
isn't too too
                        busy—

Housewife means

        married/small
        woman/container
        who/sewing
        supervises/affairs
        equipment/household

                                    —But you knew that, didn't you?

Felt it like a sick headache,
in bed, all day, wishing
for a solid noun, a better verb—

Poem with Light on Its Shoulder

—And on hers.
Though she doesn't know it,
brushing up against the private hurt:

little spur, little asterisk—

She is thinking x'd out:
smudge smudge.

She remembers someone's thumb—

And earlier, *x x o o*—
short for *I would touch you*
if I could—

Such a small idea and gone:
her hands in the air at dusk,

the sun—just a click now in the trees—

III

A little splendor is nice

—Then my need became a beautiful force.

Like gravity.

  Or the sweep of Christ's cheekbones,

   their sorrowful $x =$

Which is why I went around ruining things:

       in order to suffer   better.

Except the lesson had a hole I could put my hand through.

Like a bucket I'd carried uphill,

     —or, yes, like happiness:

  water dripping down my arms,

     the gorgeous sound of hurt leaving—

Laughter, Darkness

—Then, less:
            the middle of the end:
something like train tracks stretching
me in both directions—

            The awful whistle.

I could say *woman ocean cup*
but not quite—.

And no it did not taste metallic
                        though once I said so.

Not bittersweet either. Not fur or acrid or sex.

Of course I was hidden:
all the small breakings,

                        breaking—

    Like waves.

Like desire and restraint,
which I remember,

                    like the sigh between them,

its perfect hurt—

Wish You Were Here

Postcard of time, stolen time. And I have such wide need. How can I tell you of all the birds visiting me? First, geese at night—just as you said— flying by the light of the river. No, I mean by the absence of the light of the river. Then, cranes, three: a dream, a painting, a photograph. Also, this paper if you fold it: origami sign of—what? Good fortune against great distances, against exhaustion, or so I've read. Remember, you said you wanted birds at parting. OK then, take mine. Let this be the feather in your mailbox.

The Path from You Back to Me

Then just as suddenly the poems returned.
I had said *this red room could trap any bird,
it is so loud.*

But then it quieted.
And the bird just flew off
as though the hurt never was.

What gesture is extravagant enough now?
What better praise than *fine,
I'll take it—*

Poem of One Hand Waving

—Later the words looked less.

Like stones the lake has finished,
$$\text{that smooth.}$$

One I held was the shape of anger, one of love.

I thought to rub them together then.
I thought to leave them behind.

But I could not tell my hand from the sky:
my need the color of Sunday
$$\text{and flung wide.}$$

This is how a shore happens:

    first you walk a little distance,
$$\text{then you speak it—}$$

I Go Inside, I Go Out

Please, don't—   help is no good.

      I come when I can.

I let the quarry marks show:

this record of how
I held myself apart
      so long—

pieces of me here and there,
like a bird who isn't quick enough,
like the feather that catches and stays caught:

      a little brilliance in the bushes—

So mine is not the normal way.
      So what—?

Forward *is* difficult. Though no one told me.

Listen:
      wind through the trees means this is a frontier.

I'm right to be afraid.
Also, to go ahead.

Because *between* is a kind of hurt—

      yes, a kind of praise—

Poem with a Question in Its Pocket

The thing I thought would finish me
    now finished,

the white space I've always wanted
    shakes out

like water from my hands,

                like—

    But wait.

I have to un-poem it (crawl out) before I can poem it up again.

    It, the hurt spot.
    It, the narrative.

                  (messy messy)

Which is why I keep parentheses
handy in much the same way
you might keep bags from the grocery store:

      Would you like paper or plastic?

             the bored high school boy asks.

In case of is a good strategy here
because *Do you see how you are?* is not a real question

    though yes, it has a hook.

But who hasn't made mistakes in a "normal" day—?

It's the telling that's fraught
with *later*
just as *she loved to gather stones*
is difficult to believe.

Don't you think so
or are you impatient for the real ache,

having had enough of this foot stomping

small girl small girl

meaning, it is not smooth and who will listen—?

When the Soul Comes Out of the Body

—So then I pressed the moment a little harder
to see if what had been kept
      (lion house/meat smell/fury)
might now go free—

~

Later there were many questions such as *when exactly*
is quick over? and *why does the metallic taste of an ache*
linger? But mostly it was the problem of having used
my hands, of having tried to tame it—

~

First I thought about the hollow one way:
OK, fine, scenic.

Then I thought about it another—

~

Sometimes my mouth makes a bad noise,
like the sound of its leaving.

$$\frac{44}{45}$$

IV

I thought a little thought

When the fear cracked open,

morning had a sour smell.

Fragile was a feeling I understood then   differently.

Also, that the body has to lighten,

so that the questions might shake out—

For example, enclosure and amplification.

For example, grace:

first a small thing falls—

(thud)

then a brightening—

Plate Fragments

What happened was he dropped it and I said *save it!*
because I love an interruption:

> *you can't get there from here.*

This bird was a present we had no love for.

> (beak/neck/wing)

We kept it up high and said *go ahead, fly*

> (trunk/leaf/bare branch)

though it was porcelain and couldn't hear
our taunts or care.

But the second bird who died in our yard
was more than coincidence.

The space in the grass where it had been
was the smallest unit of meaning we knew.

Less than a word. Less than one syllable.

Less than the pet names we have for each other.

Or the sliver of plate—sky blue—that cut my hand.

Of Mixed Origin

—Interested then in the feeling of white the room

included: G next to me and the poem on a high shelf.

Sometimes I am from a place too small. Sometimes

when we talk I might as well be waving my arms

in a gesture of *up, please.* I begin to want comfort

the way I want this hybrid thing: sculpture-

orchid-poem. The question a question of how

and why: which way to this particular hunger now?

I cannot help but think what might lie down

when we lie down. There is white between

these lines. Is it fabric, lush bolt on bolt?

Is it living? I run my hand along the furrows:

the something that was here now curves from sight.

Poem without Flowers, Cranes, or Clouds

1

—Then I began to want the bad side,
to turn the poem over.

But *she had a funny little way* is a line
and not a rock,
        nothing white and wormy
in the moist spot.

Then I thought to find the mouth,
        or lip
            —red stitch—
but could not, and no wing either.

2

Words are so much is what I tell myself

though my finger wants to crook
        and part the ache
as though it is a gauzy thing

and not the sound of something closing
        (my throat)
but of something lifting off—

Against Birds, i.e., Women, i.e., Writing

Outside the world, she wore her furry collar and woolen coat
and small joy.

This was the best space despite—.

All noon, a magical situation.

The last leaves like bits of conversation she might pick up.

Her pencil dangled from a string tied to her wrist, her notebook
from a string around her neck.

Where they grooved her skin was a line she liked to trace.

Like walking by a river you have learned to love.

By a water you have named not blue not green but *animal, raw, red.*

Self-Portrait as H.D.'s Analysis with Freud

So did the fragile
from the inmost
stone's throw
into a profound
whether or not
wove
full circle
nearer to
into suffering
early, luminous
own right
my anger
though small
come out
burnt out
faceted as her
betokened as
no crown
own strange

at the seething
of abandonments
through her
let out
depth of
a Holy Day
presence of
apparent
all her fragile
object, filling
too small
translated from
like a difficult
faun-like
a swarm
is happening
between trance
night bird
safe with

the burning
as if
rare and tender
so charming
hindsight
much time
and interrupt
herself down
vessel of
inward
was late
of beloved
O God
of alchemy
and tenderness
this breathtaking
captive
to alight
locate

Dreamstuff

—Or fabric, matter: what's hung

(curtain/staircase/chasm)

between this level and the next.

Also landscape, subtle
but not gauzy like you might think.

Mine, for instance, was lion.

Not skin or fur,
but *fierce,* that energy—

~

Freud would say *latent,* meaning the real meaning
is distinct, covert—

the lion, sexual and unacceptable.

~

—Especially since the roar was a mirror.

To go *through* was the first difficulty.

(*When I caught myself listening,
I didn't like what I saw*—)

Also I suspected the other levels could tell me something

(one, a museum; one, rain)

if I let them.

~

But mostly I dreamed that the clay on the wheel would be a bowl.

(feminine thing: *there's the lip*—)

But then a head and eye
and limbs and tail.

So that the not-bowl held out its paw
as though for me to finish—

~

Of course part of me already knew.

Jung says this is *the future*

if I'm interested . . .

~

Then the inevitable *jolt*
awake: what was true

rising to the top:

a bit of white

like a flag

or

the tip of its tail—

V

There was a glimmer of it

Not expecting a miracle was the big thing.

Still, *except* was a crooked finger,

        a path of hawthorn trees

                I thought to follow—

Resistance seemed uninteresting compared to pink flowers, red fruit:

    and so—

Thus, the beginning

        though of course I didn't recognize

the voice beneath, beside mine:

        beckon beckon the sound of my breath—

Fluid, Secret, Center

—Then this interior: the most intense
between: mother and daughter: each,

a lung, impossibly delicate and essential,
the twin held breath nearly bursting

like the womb, floral organ where I was,
once— But we don't mention this

or the little fists that tendrilled up,
exploding, or earlier, the blue green hum

beneath her hum: the first thing
and vaguely salty, newly mine.

Egyptology and Demolition

Some days she is all sky motion, or
her mouth is, moving toward
everything and . . . Sunday is so far gone,
so swallowed and she is all *good-bye house,
good-bye very best cat*—

This is what she loves, this
lying in river water, in decay and *just think
of what might have been here once. . .*

—as in Egypt where
archeologists couldn't help but rush
in, feeding tombs dynamite as though
it was hard candy—so good, so
not-so-good all at once—

Who can resist that kind of happiness—Oh!—
though it hurts the way the taste of lemons
hurts, makes her want less
then more, the same way
her new breasts ache when she runs.

Aside

—That no one hears.
For example, the girl in the bedroom who nobody wanted.

Yes, flinch.
To turn away is cruel and natural.

     (Also, to remember wanting—)

Thus, the origin of parentheses, the let's keep it
clandestine and essential:

     (his mouth *right there*—)

Surely, you understand the need to put.

For example, yourself
              or
                 leftovers,
the happy happy snap of Tupperware
like a promise, like tomorrow
                    kept.

Which is not quite the same *kept*
as when you were in the daughter space

     (remember—?
     shape of longing,
     shape of a pear
     ripening: some
     yellow, some
     green   still)

Or as when you dreamt *may I?*
and velocity—

(his hands—yes, please—his tongue)

But the point here is—what

exactly?

That the girl was a curve

(That you were)

That she was also upright

(That you tried *so hard*)

And *Can you be very sure?*

For instance, this syntactical structure.
Are you in it now?

Or have you digressed?

(You know, gone off

with him)

Have you surprised yourself quietly?

Another Glacier Museum

—But things never did quite turn out how you imagined,

did they? Even the words that once felt so good

in your mouth (the very definition of a poem) let you down.

It was just that you had so much invested in right

outcomes. Of course touch was your first love (Oh—

to have a body again!) but *later* kept interfering—

What was there to do but find an even colder thing

than you at seven—remember?—you all bundled up,

all scarf and mittens, just doing what they said, just

keeping to yourself, and going along—

Fabric/Lyric

Unable to reconcile myself,
I let the idea out:

    here is the space I've cleared, the poem
    not yet come,

        though it might:

    three-dimensional, back-lit, hung—

And stunning, a thing to want to cut
and wear: as in,

    I could live with this against my skin—

Touch is crucial,
                an attention I would like to pay,

    but I cannot word
    the invitation right: my hands

        flutter, drop.

I say *gauzy* the way you might say *love*,
meaning *my hunger*—

    desire a net, after all,

                and rigged—

though I am the one hopping

      —right foot, left foot—

    there is no other body here:

After (thought

Even when I try not to think of *it*.

Even when I try not to think.

For example, this still nice space

     (so possible—

but right away I go *inside*, I go
—almost—parenthetical.

Except the right one is trouble. is gone.

     (curving out of sight

I wish it would just
bracket. or yoke. or
somehow decide
to contain this animal—

   ~

I'm thinking of bears, mostly.

     (I am saying this for the first time

polar bears which can be so

     (I am writing this on a too small piece of paper

cute on TV, so human
the way they hide
their noses, covering them with snow

the very thing he did,
all hiding and hidden and

(metaphorically speaking, of course

all *snowy*—

~

Like this too small and too large page
both at once and not nice now

(so white—which way is finished?

Or like these parentheses:
the left one trying, the right
one refusing.

(this is not that kind of animal

~

So there's a draft now.

(meaning *I tried*, meaning *error*
I wish I could just
blow away like an eyelash:

(*hold still, just let me—*

or keep, like a snowflake on an eyelash
on a person I once loved—

~

But you're getting cold, aren't you?

(you're wondering

Shall I close it then?

Shall I contain it?

(saying *oh well. tra la.*

saying *here. I'm fine. really.*

come. it's done. sit by me.)

VI

This is sweet too—

So this is *finally*:

        the part that wanted to break

                broke.

You could not not let it.

Take your hands from your ears:

        the dish cracked and cracked and stopped.

Why bother?   Forget the broom. Step away.

    Yes—   like that.

You can sigh now if you want.

        You can say *yes* and mean it.

Wish Book

—Except not that shape or weight.

Not the Sears catalog, pictures of dolls.

    (*click click* go the eyes I loved)

Not a house. Not a girl.

    (porch light shimmer)

Not a key. Not bending down to pick it up.

Not ever.

But inside—

    Martha Graham said *the lonely place.*
    Martha Graham said *between your thighs.*

    Meaning, *if this is what you really want—*
    Meaning, *twinkle twinkle—*

So I said I would.

Then even my knees and elbows got so light!

    (what had been hinged—)

Then each hand I waved

    or that once waved to me

        began receding—

Hula Girl

This is the girl with a bird at each hip.
I mean, each hip is a bird disguised
as the way she moves without trying.
Effortless, her hands at her hair, her hair
curled behind her ear. Just so, she occupies
her space and a little of yours, too.
All afternoon the afternoon loves her.
All night she closes her mouth around
the smallest sounds, pulls her legs up close.

The Art of Kissing

The first lesson is electricity.
The second, *Attention, gentlemen—*

Or at least it was in 1936
in the book of *How.*

Unless of course you were *the girl*
in question—

                              (unless you were hedging)

But the truth was I wanted him to.

Even though kisses shouldn't be free.

                        (my mother told me)
Even though love is dirty.

                        (she yelled when I was ten)

But he possessed *the same gentleness*
as would a cat
lifting her precious kittens
and touched my face
just like the book said.

                    (mew mew)

This was what she never once mentioned: the *sex-hunger,*

never said white space
                    fish mouth
                              which way please please—

But gradually—

So pretext was unnecessary:

    After all, we were not the book's shy couple
    and not hers either.

Though, yes, we sat on the sofa.

                        (yes, there was a quiver—)

Structure and Surface

—At last my hands have found a world,
a landscape where they are faces, looking up,

or sky, down, depending on where I stand
and how the fabric hangs—

Here, needles punch through to entangle,
to collage and blur the outline of what was.

The selvage edge means I may ravel,
but this one—deep sea—will not.

How is it cloth can be water and hung
dripping like a rope of kelp to climb?

Or hollow as bamboo cut down, each thread
a stalk and music a mouth might sound?

Such cloth, sculpted or layered, undulates
like ocean or forest, like flesh: articulate terrain.

Tilde

Little body, swell—,
                    can I borrow you,
                    can I make the shape?

~

—like that one, lying down

      (*like you,* he says,

                    pointing—)

~

Sometimes he's quiet as painting I have loved:

      soft grids of white on white—

~

As I suspected, *the diacritical mark*
indicates *special value.*

      ~

—some of his were jaunty,
            like the stick we cleaned for marshmallows;
      some, serpentine,
like the wall around the convent—

      ~

Of course the quick jab bad distance
was contained there too and unavoidable.

~

—but when he used his riverbed voice,
I agreed to walk along . . .

~

Dear *between, hesitation,*

     are you light?

          (I'm feeling my way—)

     are you fine?

~

Mostly, that after the white space, we would begin—

for G.

Inside the Yellow Dress (2)

—This is the desire I spoke of. Air articulate with *plenty*, each leaf a word and good. Even the ones that fall send up light. This one has a hole: pin prick, or camera, or throat. To get through, language folds down smaller than all the body's small hairs, smaller than the pores on the skin: smaller even than *touch*, the one stunning syllable all our mouths crave.

Notes

The book takes its title from a painting by Nancy Brett.

The quote from Ann Hamilton's *whitecloth* comes from a 1999 exhibition at The Aldrich Museum of Contemporary Art.

"When the Soul Comes Out of the Body" was written in response to Brenda Hillman, who asks good questions. The italicized line in "Poem Without Flowers, Cranes, or Clouds" comes from her as well.

The title "Against Birds, i.e. Women, i.e. Writing" is borrowed from Helene Cixous' *Three Steps on the Ladder of Writing*.

"Self-Portrait as H.D.'s Analysis with Freud" owes a debt of gratitude to Naomi Ruth Lowinsky's "Our Lady of the Pomegranate."

I discovered the information about Martha Graham that appears in "Wish Book" in Susan Leigh Foster's *Reading Dancing*.

"The Art of Kissing" was inspired by a book of the same title published in 1936.

"Structure and Surface" and the other fabric poems were inspired by a Japanese textile exhibit at the Museum of Modern Art, New York, 1998-99.

Acknowledgements

Many thanks to the editors of the publications where the following poems first appeared:

American Letters & Commentary: "Poem of One Hand Waving"

Controlled Burn: "Poem with a Riddle in It"

Defined Providence: "Wish You Were Here"

Green Mountains Review: "Egyptology and Demolition,"
  "Laughter, Darkness," "Self-Portrait as an Animal Skinned and Hung"

Hubbub: "November," "Poem without Flowers,
  Cranes, or Clouds"

The Kenyon Review: "Moving Away from an Event"

Mississippi Review: "Tilde"

The Ohio Review: "Poem with Light on Its Shoulder"

Pleiades: "After (thought," "Aside"

Quarterly West: "Fabric/Lyric"

Third Coast: "Inside the Yellow Dress"

The Virginia Quarterly Review: "When the Soul Comes Out of the Body"

The White Pine Review: "Hula Girl"

"The Art of Kissing" and "Poem with Light on Its Shoulder" also appeared in *American Poetry: The Next Generation*, ed. Gerald Costanzo and Jim Daniels, Carnegie Mellon University Press, 2000.

Thanks to my father for his support; to Rebecca Roberts, wonderful writer and reader and fellow worker in the comma mines; as always, to Ellen, a girl in a yellow dress (once); to Danielle Cordaro and Cressida Madigan, two of my favorite writers. Above all, gratitude and much love to my husband, Gerry LaFemina.

Thanks also to ArtServe Michigan and the Michigan Council for the Arts and Cultural Affairs for a Creative Artist Grant that assisted in the completion of these poems.

photo by Sue Varady

Mary Ann Samyn is the author of two prize-winning collections of poetry: *Rooms by the Sea*, 1994 Kent State University Press/Wick Chapbook selection, and *Captivity Narrative*, 1999 Ohio State University Press/*The Journal* award winner. She is a graduate of the creative writing programs at Ohio University, and The University of Virginia where she held a Hoyns Fellowship. Her work has appeared in *Denver Quarterly*, *Field*, *The Kenyon Review*, *Quarterly West*, *The Ohio Review*, *Verse*, and elsewhere.

New Issues Poetry & Prose

Editor, Herbert Scott

James Armstrong, *Monument in a Summer Hat*
Michael Burkard, *Pennsylvania Collection Agency*
Anthony Butts, *Fifth Season*
Gladys Cardiff, *A Bare Unpainted Table*
Joseph Featherstone, *Brace's Cove*
Lisa Fishman, *The Deep Heart's Core Is a Suitcase*
Robert Grunst, *The Smallest Bird in North America*
Mark Halperin, *Time as Distance*
Myronn Hardy, *Approaching the Center*
Edward Haworth Hoeppner, *Rain Through High Windows*
Janet Kauffman, *Rot (fiction)*
Josie Kearns, *New Numbers*
Maurice Kilwein Guevara, *Autobiography of So-and-so: Poems in Prose*
Ruth Ellen Kocher, *When the Moon Knows You're Wandering*
Steve Langan, *Freezing*
Lance Larsen, *Erasable Walls*
David Dodd Lee, *Downsides of Fish Culture*
Deanne Lundin, *The Ginseng Hunter's Notebook*
Joy Manesiotis, *They Sing to Her Bones*
David Marlatt, *A Hog Slaughtering Woman*
Paula McLain, *Less of Her*
Sarah Messer, *Bandit Letters*
Malena Mörling, *Ocean Avenue*
Julie Moulds, *The Woman with a Cubed Head*
Marsha de la O, *Black Hope*
C. Mikal Oness, *Water Becomes Bone*
Elizabeth Powell, *The Republic of Self*
Margaret Rabb, *Granite Dives*
Rebecca Reynolds, *Daughter of the Hangnail*
Martha Rhodes, *Perfect Disappearance*
Beth Roberts, *Brief Moral History in Blue*
John Rybicki, *Traveling at High Speeds*
Mary Ann Samyn, *Inside the Yellow Dress*
Mark Scott, *Tactile Values*
Diane Seuss-Brakeman, *It Blows You Hollow*
Marc Sheehan, *Greatest Hits*
Sarah Jane Smith, *No Thanks- and other stories (fiction)*
Phillip Sterling, *Mutual Shores*
Angela Sorby, *Distance Learning*